Ethics Made Easy

Ethics Made Easy

Les Livingstone
MBA, Ph.D. CPA (NY & TX)

<u>Dedication</u>

To my wife Trudy, with lots of love.

What lies behind us and what lies ahead of us are tiny matters compared to what lies within us.

Walt Emerson

Ethics Made Easy

If I am not for myself, who will be for me?
And if I am only for myself, what am I?
And if not now, when?

Rabbi Hillel (30 B.C.-9 A.D.)

It takes 20 years to build a reputation and five minutes to ruin it. If you think about that, you'll do things differently.

Warren Buffett

Introduction

Our lives bring up one ethical issue after another. Ethical choices face us in many of our everyday decisions. The way that we make these decisions has great influence on our futures and the futures of those affected by our decisions. There are repeated ethical scandals in business, in politics and every other area of human activity. In these ethical scandals people of wealth, of achievement, and of prominent status have lost their good reputations and endured public disgrace. Some have faced criminal trials or have incurred

4

significant financial losses. Some have even gone to prison. They, and their families, have been ruined. If they had it to do over again, how many of these people would make the same ethical choices that led to their humiliation? What can we learn from their bitter experiences?

The unmistakable lesson is that ethical choices matter a great deal, and that ethical lapses can have drastic unforeseen consequences. It is abundantly clear that ethics is vitally important to all of us. In this book, we attempt to create a practical framework for ethical decision making.

Law and Ethics

Some people may ask what difference, if any, is there between ethics, on the one hand, and law, on the other hand. Most often, laws express valid ethical principles. But this is not invariably the case. Occasionally laws can be immoral. For example, in certain U.S. states slavery was legal for most of the 19th century. Joseph Stalin sent political dissenters to Siberia and to their deaths under laws prevailing in the Soviet Union at the time. Under German law at the time, Hitler sent millions to their deaths in Nazi concentration camps for the crime of being Jews or Gypsies or for having physical or mental disabilities. So ethics and the law most often run parallel, but there can occasionally also be deviations between them.

Ethical Relativism

Speaking of deviations, some people maintain that moral beliefs and practices vary from culture to culture. Indeed, some people say that moral beliefs and practices even vary within a given culture from person to person. These beliefs are referred to as ethical relativism. There is no doubt that differing moral beliefs and practices exist in different cultures and different persons as a factual matter. For example, news reports state that slavery is still practiced in a few parts of the world. Also, bribery is commonplace in many parts of the world.

In these circumstances, are there any absolute standards of ethics that apply universally, independent of cultural or personal beliefs and practices? Or are ethics simply whatever is currently believed or practiced by various cultures or persons? In that case, there are no ethical standards and ethics becomes nothing more than a menu of endless open choices, all choices being equally valid.

To answer these important questions we need to distinguish between descriptive and prescriptive approaches. A descriptive approach simply reports what is observed. It is neutral, imposing no standards, applying no criteria, and making no judgments. Examples would be the descriptive observations of anthropologists about the beliefs and practices of different cultures, and the research conducted by psychologists on different individuals and personality types. On the other hand, a prescriptive approach seeks out absolute standards and universal criteria that apply to all cultures and all persons.

An example of a prescriptive approach is the Ten Commandments, which makes no exceptions for different cultures or different persons. In contrast to a descriptive approach, a prescriptive approach inherently requires absolute standards and universal criteria. In contrast to ethical relativism, which imposes no standards or criteria and regards all ethical choices as equally valid, a prescriptive approach rejects the notions that all ethical choices are equally valid and are contingent upon cultural and personal factors. A prescriptive approach demands moral absolutes and establishes a single moral compass for all cultures, for all people and for all seasons. A prescriptive approach denies Moral Nihilism (the view that right and wrong do not exist) and Moral Skepticism (doubt about whether right and wrong exist).

Practical Solutions

As we have just seen, ethical philosophy can be complex and abstract. It can, and often does, lead to highly theoretical debates between experts over points that seem remote, perplexing, or even

7

trivial. We have no desire to add fuel to this fire. Rather, we prefer to avoid these arcane debates in favor of practical solutions. Our framework uses the major mainstream contributions of ethical philosophy, but is sufficiently clear and concise to be used and useful for practical day-to-day purposes. At the same time, the framework should not become so simplistic or crude that it ends up as superficial.

A Universal Rule

Ethical philosophy has evolved over many centuries. If we turn to the earliest writings on ethics, we repeatedly see one central principle that keeps on appearing in many different sources.

> Buddhism: 560 BC, from the Udanavarga 5:18- "Hurt not others with that which pains yourself."

> Christianity: 30 AD, from the King James Version, 7:12- "Whatsoever ye would that others should do to you, do ye even so to them."

> Confucianism: 557 BC, from the Analects 15:23- "What you do not want done to yourself, do not do to others."

8

Hinduism: 3200 BC, from the Hitopadesa- "One should always treat others as they themselves wish to be treated."

Islam: circa 620 AD, Sunnah, from the Koran- "No one of you is a believer until he desires for his brother that which he desires for himself."

Jainism: circa 500 BC, from Agamas, Sutrakrtanga 1.10, 1-3- "One should treat all beings as he himself would be treated."

Judaism: 1300 BC, from the Old Testament, Leviticus 19:18- "Thou shalt Love thy neighbor as thyself."

 Zoroastrianism: 600 BC, from the Shast-na-shayast 13:29- "Whatever is disagreeable to yourself, do not do unto others."

This principle is known to us as the Golden Rule. It is the fundamental principle of many religions, and it is widely venerated as the highest standard of ethical conduct. This principle is also the foundation of the ethical framework of the great moral philosopher Immanuel Kant (1724-1804).

Ethics As Duty

Immanuel Kant began by asking: "what is basically good, without any qualification?" He rejected answers such as the following:

"happiness" (because deserving people may be unhappy, and likewise undeserving people may be happy),

"courage" (because courage in a villain will simply make him more of a villain),

"loyalty" (because it may be lent to a bad cause), and

"charity" (because it also may be given to a bad cause). These qualities may all be good, but they are not good without qualification.

To Kant, the only quality that is good without qualification is *deontology*. Deontology does not just mean good intentions. It is "... not a mere wish, but the summoning of all means in our power ..." to perform what is our duty. Therefore Kant's *theory of moral goodness* is that we do our duty. Note that "duty" is not necessarily doing just what we are inclined to do. Kant is distrustful of human desire or feelings as a moral guide. Kant's concept of duty is doing what we *ought* to do, not simply what we *desire* to do.

In that case, what is our duty? This leads to Kant's *theory of moral obligation.* Kant argues that what sets human beings apart from all other living creatures is that we are the only creatures that are *rational*. If our purpose in life had been merely to please our senses (hedonism) or to be happy, then nature would not have endowed us with our unique powers of reasoning. Simple animal instinct would have equipped us far better than reason to pursue sensual pleasures or happiness.

The good person then acts from reason rather than feelings, says Kant. This distinction is important, because feelings can differ from person to person. But if we all correctly follow reason, then we should all reach the same conclusion. That makes reason *universal* to all humans, and UNIVERSALITY is what Kant insists upon in ethics. Why?

　　　11

Universality

Universality means applicable to every person, without any exception. It is how to determine whether an act is right or wrong. For instance, consider stealing. If I steal from you, would I be equally willing for everyone to steal (including, of course, stealing from me)? In that case, stealing would become universal. Everyone would steal, and private property would cease to exist. Certainly I would be unwilling for stealing to become universal. Therefore stealing does not have universality, and that is why it is unethical to steal. For the same reason murder, armed robbery, rape, arson, and fraud do not have universality. Therefore they too are not ethical.

Kant noted that universality is equivalent to acting with respect for all persons. In other words:

1. Universality makes an act right, or that the lack of universality makes an act wrong
2. Respect for persons makes an act right, or that the lack of respect for persons makes an act wrong.

This theory expresses the very essence of morality. To act ethically is to act on a universal principle. Stated as respect for persons, ethics recognizes the innate human dignity of every person. According to Kant, our duty is to follow the rule of universality, or respect for all persons. That is the ultimate result of his theory of moral obligation, and it is stated in Kant's categorical imperative.

A Categorical Imperative

Kant stated his categorical imperative as follows:

> "Hence there is only one categorical imperative and it is this: Act only according to that maxim whereby you can at the same time will that it should become a universal law"

This principle is very specific. It requires these precise steps:

1. Define the particular act under consideration;
2. Derive the underlying maxim for the act;
3. Test the maxim as a universal law.

Here is an example to illustrate these steps. A person in need is forced to borrow money. She knows that she will not get a loan unless she promises to repay it. She also knows that she will not be able to repay the loan. Suppose she still decides to borrow the money.

Working through the above steps:

1.   Define the act: to borrow on her promise to repay.

2.   Derive the underlying maxim: Since I need money, I will borrow on my false promise to repay.

3.   Test the maxim as a universal law: What if everyone in need could validly make false promises? Then all promises would become worthless.

Therefore breaking a promise is unethical. The essence of a universal law is that one cannot make an exception just for oneself. The exception destroys the universality of the law.   Kant expressed the same principle in terms of the respect for persons:

> "Act in such a way that you treat humanity, whether in your own person or in the person of another, always at the same time as an end and never simply as a means"

This principle requires respect for all persons, including oneself. If a person is treated only as a means, that person is merely used as an object, and not respected as a human being with innate dignity. Treating a person as an end, rather than a means, requires respect for their human worth.

Why is universality equivalent to respecting persons as ends and not merely means? When the principle of universality is violated, it is by making an exception for oneself. For example, what if I can steal but I do not approve of other people stealing? If I steal, then I am treating my victim as a means, and not as an end. This also violates the principle of respect for persons. Therefore the two different forms of the principle are equivalent.

Conversely, if I treat someone only as a means, their will or end is ignored. If this is made universal, then my will should also to be ignored. But how could I will that to become a universal law? Again, it is clear that the two different forms of the principle are equivalent.

Now, consider the 'respect for persons" form of Kant's principle. Apply it to the previous example of a woman in need who borrows on a false promise to repay. The woman making a false promise is using the lender as merely a means to her own end. The lender could not possibly share the borrower's end of obtaining money under false pretences. Therefore this borrowing is unethical, because it is in violation of universality, and it also violates the "respect for persons."

Kant defines his principle as a *"categorical imperative"*. An imperative is an order, like "ready, aim, fire!" A categorical imperative allows no deviation: it is a direct command. Kant's imperative commands that we do the right thing every single time, not just usually, or just when it happens to be convenient. That makes it a duty.

What Kant has prescribed as the categorical imperative is, of course, equivalent to the Golden Rule. Versions of the Golden Rule existed for more than twenty-four centuries before Kant was born. He did not create the Golden Rule. But he worked out the rigorous step by step formal logic that leads to it, and he added to it respect for self as well as others. In essence, Kant's contribution was to fully universalize the Golden Rule.

Applying Kant's Ethics of Duty

Now that we have covered the basic elements of Kant's theory, we are ready to apply it to a business decision. Kim is being interviewed by Tom as a possible consultant to the City in negotiating a new electric contract. Kim asks for a fee of $1,600 per day for an estimated 10 days of consulting work, for a total fee of $16,000. Tom for undisclosed reasons counters with a surprising offer of a $30,000 fee,. But he then requests Kim to give back $14,000 to the "flower fund."

He explains that the flower fund helps the mayor deal with hardship cases among City employees, whom he says are underpaid and receive meager health benefits. The mayor wishes to be perceived as a caring and compassionate politician. Kim asks Tom if this contribution of $14,000 is an absolute requirement for her to get the consulting assignment. Tom ambiguously replies: "You do whatever you want, and I'll do whatever I must."

Kim is torn in two different ways as she considers her decision. On the one hand, she ardently desires the consulting experience and sees that it can get her started on a successful consulting career. The fee will also be welcome, to improve her financial position. On the other hand, Kim feels uncomfortable with Tom's unexpected request for the flower fund contribution, even though it may perhaps be a worthy cause. She also feels used, in helping to deceive the public by agreeing to an apparent $30,000 fee in order to further the Mayor's political purposes, when it is clear that her actual fee will be only $16,000.

How can Kant's ethical theory help in guiding Kim's decision? The categorical imperative says:

> "Act only according to that maxim whereby you can at the same time will that it should become a universal law"

Kim must consider how she would feel as a city resident, as a taxpayer, and as a voter if consultants to City Hall agreed to highly inflated fees just to help the Mayor's political image. If Kim, as a citizen, believes that this is unethical, then Kim as a consultant is being unethical to accept Tom's offer.

Using the detailed steps:

1. <u>Define the act:</u> obtain the assignment by agreeing to a deceptive $30,000 fee;

2. <u>Derive the underlying maxim:</u> I want this assignment, so 1 will agree to a deceptive fee to help mislead the voters about the Mayor's image;

3. <u>Test the maxim as a universal law.</u> What if everyone wanting business from the City conspired with City Hall to deceive the voters? Then they would be party to lying: Lying is not acceptable as a universal law because if lying became pervasive, then no one would believe anyone else, and truth

would cease to exist. Therefore this rule is unethical, and Kim should not make herself an exception to the universal law.

Note that it is the <u>maxim</u> or <u>rule</u> rather than the act that is tested for universality. Kant maintains that it is the basic underlying rationale that determines what is ethical, rather than the deed itself. Universality sets the standard for morality. For example, the woman in need who borrows based on a false promise to repay is not unethical because she borrows, or because she promises to repay. These are only the acts, not the rule. She is unethical because she follows a rule which she would not wish to be universal.

We can also apply the equivalent "respect for persons" form of Kant's categorical imperative to Kim's decision:

> "Act in such a way that you treat humanity, whether in your own person or in the person of another, always at the same time as an end and never simply as a means"

Kim should ask herself if she is treating the residents of the City only as a means to win the consulting assignment, or also as an end in themselves. Kim's answer is that she could not be serving the interests of the City residents by helping to deceive them. Then it is unethical to accept the assignment.

By applying Kant's theory, Kim is clearly able to see that the ethical decision is to refuse the assignment. Of course, it is then up to her to be ethical or not. That is the test of her willingness to do her ethical duty. The theory has guided Kim to the ethical choice, and that moral guidance is precisely what the theory has to offer.

It is worth pointing out again an aspect of the categorical imperative, when it is stated in the form of respect for persons:

> "Act in such a way that you treat humanity, whether in your own person or in the person of another, always at the same time as an end and never simply as a means."

Note that it commands respect for one's own human dignity, as well as that of other persons. Recall that Kim felt "used" by the mayor for political purposes. According to Kant, it is not ethical to allow oneself to be only a means to another person's ends. To let oneself be treated only as a means is to deny one's own human dignity.

In applying Kant's theory to this case, we see that it does not provide a specifically tailored course of action for us to follow. For example, it does not give the readymade answer to Kim of either accepting or refusing the assignment. It does not make the decision for us. Instead, it gives us the critical question to ask so that we can determine what the ethical course of action is. This key question is, of course, the one posed in the categorical imperative (in whichever of its two forms we select).

In other words, Kant has given us an ethical signpost. Like all signposts, it points out the correct direction. But it cannot also take us to where we want to go. That part is up to us. In the real world, with its many complex and difficult ethical decisions, a reliable signpost is most valuable.

Another issue for Kim is what moral responsibility she may have in relation to the mayor's scheme. Does she ignore it, talk to the mayor, or report it to the news media or to the relevant law enforcement agency? We will consider these alternatives, starting with ignoring it:.

1.   Define the act: ignore the mayor's scheme.

2.   Derive the underlying maxim: I will ignore it because it is not my business.

3.   Test the maxim as a universal law: what if everyone ignored the

transgressions that they
witnessed?

If all transgressions go unreported, as a universal law, then many more transgressions will be ignored. Transgression will be encouraged. For example, how would Kim feel if she were attacked on the street and all the other people on the street ignore her attacker? No one intervenes or calls the police. The rule does not pass the test of universality in this case.

A more technical way of stating this is: the reason corruption may persist is because the corrupt person ignores the laws restraining other people. This allows the corrupt person to benefit from ignoring the laws. However, if all people ignored corruption because it was not their business (if, in other words, the underlying rule "I will ignore it because it is not my business" is universalized), corruption would become increasingly widespread.

Therefore it is ethical for Kim to become a whistleblower. She should blow the whistle to the mayor, the press or the legal authorities. But, whichever of these parties she chooses, there is a problem. We appear to have mixed feelings about whistleblowers. Some of us believe that it is disloyal or unfair to blow the whistle, for example, on an employer. As a practical matter, the whistleblower has not always been well respected or well treated in America. Cases of whistle blowing are notoriously difficult to resolve.

In all probability the mayor is the first person that Kim should talk with. If he would end this practice, the situation could be mended. But what if he does not agree? Then the conversation could end any chance Kim may have to ever work for the city. If Kim then goes to the press or a law enforcement agency, she may not only lose her chance to work for the city, but she may find it difficult to get work from any organization. Whistleblowers are not always welcomed elsewhere.

Kim has a conflict of interest. More exactly, her self interest and her ethical duty may be on a collision course. While the ethical responsibility is clear, the personal costs may be high. Kim will have to make a decision one way or the other. Having considered Kant's signposts, however, she will at least be able to judge the ethics of her alternatives. Whether she chooses ethics over her other motivations is up to her.

Kant's theory has been criticized as being incomplete or inconsistent. For example, some critics say that it does not satisfactorily deal with conflicting duties. But it is generally respected and widely accepted as one of the leading ethical theories. It is the main <u>deontological</u> theory (from

23

the Greek "deon": which means duty or obligation).

Deontological theories take a "yes or no" approach: either an act is ethical, or it is not ethical. There are no shades of grey in between the black and the white. In addition to the deontological theories, there are teleological theories (from the Greek "telos", meaning objective or purpose).

Teleological Theories

In contrast to the "either or" deontological theories, the teleological theories measure ethics along a continuous scale, like a ruler. A particular act may have more ethical value than another act, so the teleological method seeks out the act with the maximum ethical value. The main teleological theory is the utilitarian approach. This theory too is generally accepted, in a variety of forms, and respected. At the same time, it is also subject to criticism and can be regarded as incomplete.

The utilitarian theory was developed by the British philosophers Jeremy Bentham (1748-1832) and John Stuart Mill (1805-1873). It can be described as follows.

Like Kant, the utilitarians start out with the subject of good. They ask: whose good must the ethical theory consider? On the principle of universality, it cannot be just the good of the decision-maker. It must be the good of other persons too. In that case how can we stop short of the good of everyone, or "the general good"?

Then it is ethical to promote the greatest possible general good. So the maximization of the general good is the main purpose of ethics, according to the utilitarian theory. More specifically, the most ethical act is the one that produces the most good. The difference between right and wrong is entirely the amount of good produced. For example, telling the truth is good, because it is useful to everyone as a whole to rely on the word of others. Lies are bad because they create general distrust and insecurity, and they invite retaliation. Stealing is bad, because it violates the valuable social institution of private property ownership, and it also creates distrust and insecurity, and invites retaliation. Bentham's famous saying was "the greatest good for the greatest number (of people)". But this creates a measurement problem: just what do we mean by "the greatest number?"

A Measurement Problem

If some act will benefit three persons, how do we measure its usefulness? We must measure, because the utilitarian theory requires us to do the act which maximizes benefit. Unless we measure the good of each alternative act, we do not know which act is the most beneficial.

Bentham suggested that each human being "counts for one". It is like the democratic principle of "one person, one vote". That sounds good: let's say the act in question has a benefit measure of 3, because it benefits three people. Now say the alternative act only benefits two persons. Then the first act must be better, it would seem.

But imagine that the first act added $100 to the income of each of the three beneficiaries, for a total of $300. Now imagine that the alternative act added $200 to the income of each of its two beneficiaries, for a total of $400. In this case which act is better: act A, which benefits three persons, or act B, which benefits only two persons? If each person "counts for one" act A must be better. But act A only adds $300 to the combined incomes of the three persons, while act B adds total income of $400 to the two persons concerned. In money measurement, act B is very much better. The previous result is reversed. Everything depends on how benefits are measured. This problem gets more complex if some persons benefit and other persons lose (get negative benefits). How do we measure the net total benefits now?

In brief, utilitarianism involves a cost-benefit calculation. It is well-known that in cost-benefit analysis it is often very difficult to measure the costs and benefits, and even more difficult to add together the benefits of some persons and the losses of others. This problem of measuring benefits is familiar to experts, but they do not have a full solution to it. That is a weakness of the utilitarian theory.

But there is a partial solution. This solution will work as long as all persons involved will benefit (after deducting their costs from their benefits) or at least none will lose. In this special case, the most ethical action can be identified. This is known as a "Pareto--optimal" solution, named after the economist Vilfredo Pareto who developed the concept. More precisely, an action is considered to be Pareto-optimal if, and only if, there is no alternative to the proposed solution that could make everyone better off and no one worse off.

Using Utilitarian Ethics

In order to try our hand at using the utilitarian approach, we flash back again to Kim at City Hall. How does utilitarianism guide her decision whether to accept the consulting assignment?

We must consider the costs and benefits to all parties who are involved. These costs and benefits are listed in the table below.

Parties	Costs	Benefits	Benefits Less Costs
Kim	Feeling of being used. Time & effort	Consulting experience. $16,000 fee	Positive
City Hall	$16,000 fee	Consulting service	Positive
Mayor	None	Political advantage	Positive
City Residents	Deception on fee. Add $30,000 to bills	None	Negative but Minor

Table of Costs and Benefits

Some of the costs and benefits listed above are easy to understand. But some need to be explained, as follows. Kim's consulting fee is shown as a benefit to her. But is this correct? After all she is putting in time and effort to earn the fee. Is this not just a straight exchange? True, but she would not trade her time and her effort in exchange for the fee if she did not regard this as a beneficial trade. Of course, Kim's benefit is less than her full $16,000 fee because she does have to contribute her time and effort to the assignment. But clearly the net gain is large enough to persuade her to make the trade.

This is the economic basis of all voluntary transactions. The exchange is made because both sides benefit from it. Otherwise the transaction would not take place. When a willing buyer and a willing seller make an exchange, with neither under duress, the result is Pareto-optimal because both of them benefit. That is in fact why they have agreed to the transaction. Therefore the City also benefits from Kim's services, even after payment of her $16,000 fee.

The city may pay the full $30,000 amount of the proposed consulting fee. But most likely it will recover this outlay by adding it to the tax base. Therefore, to the city, the costs equal the benefits so far as the $30,000 payment is concerned.

The residents of the City, however, would pay an extra $30,000 in taxes over the lifetime of the consulting contract. Also, they must bear the non-monetary cost of being deceived about the padded $30,000 consulting fee. It can be argued that an extra $30,000 in taxes spread over the City's entire population is negligible. Certainly the cost per taxpayer could only amount to an extra penny or so. It can also be argued that the deception by the Mayor is very minor. After all, don't we expect politicians to indulge in some puffery, and don't we take their statements with a grain of salt, to allow for their evident self-interest? So the total costs to the City in this case may be minimal.

What about Kim's feeling of being used? How serious a matter is it really? In a year's time, chances are that she may not even care about it. So the total cost to Kim could be minimal too. If the costs to all parties involved are probably slight, what of the benefits? The benefits to all are definitely not minor. Kim gains, some of the Mayor's unfortunate staff will gain and the Mayor gains.

Although there is no Pareto-optimal solution (since taxpayers seem to incur costs and no benefits and are therefore slightly worse off), it seems that the total benefits nonetheless substantially exceed the total costs in this case. Therefore the utilitarian approach could provide ethical justification for Kim to accept the offer. Kim receives $30,000, less the $14,000 for the flower fund, so she gains $16,000. The City pays out $30,000 instead of $16,000, but the extra $14,000 cost to the City benefits other parties (i.e., the mayor and employees of City Hall) by the full amount of $14,000. City taxpayers are worse off, but, in each case, by a minimal amount.

So from a utilitarian view, the costs and benefits to the City cancel out, and Kim is much better off than any taxpayer is worse off. The ethical decision for Kim is to go ahead and accept the Mayor's offer. Are you surprised? Does this decision really seem ethical to you? We will take a closer look at this situation below.

Are Utilitarian Decisions Really Ethical?

The decision for Kim to go ahead with the inflated consulting fee can apparently be justified by using utilitarian ethical reasoning. Although it is not Pareto-optimal, the decision seems to do more good for Kim than it does harm to anyone else. This is the kind of issue that is often raised to criticize the utilitarian approach. Similar issues raised by critics of utilitarianism usually involve cases where the greatest benefit for a majority of persons is obtainable only by penalizing a minority, or some innocent victim. By emphasizing this unfair victimization, critics of utilitarianism try to show that utilitarian principles conflict with our strongest moral values.

For example, consider Robin Hood and his merry men, the bandits of Sherwood Forest. They robbed the idle rich to help the deserving poor. A utilitarian would say that Robin Hood was acting ethically. He used little or no violence to harm his rich victims, and they were so wealthy that they scarcely missed what he stole from them. The poor benefited greatly from his help, because they were destitute and severely oppressed.

But is it not wrong to steal, even from the wealthy? It goes against our deeply-held moral convictions to suggest that the fundamental rights of one group, in this case the wealthy, can be violated in the name of another group, in this instance the poor. If utilitarianism is going to be a viable ethical theory, it must be sure to uphold this moral consideration.

In fact, it does so. Critics who make this kind of accusation overlook the basic principle that is at the heart of utilitarianism. According to this principle, we must consider not only the persons immediately affected by a particular decision, but also all persons who are indirectly affected by the moral consequences of that decision. So consider what happens if the act is repeated again and again. Soon everyone is stealing from the rich to give to the poor. Then morals are being corrupted. The word getting out encourages other people to act unethically, because they see others gaining unfairly and morals becoming lax. Utilitarianism, because it promotes the greater good of everyone, could not condone such a situation. So the criticism of utilitarianism is flawed. Utilitarianism does not give Robin Hood an ethical license to steal.

Now we see that utilitarian ethics require that Kim should refuse the offer of consulting from the city. Apparently, flower fund contributions and therefore political deceptions are everyday business at City Hall. If Kim accepts the offer then she is unethically adding to the pattern of corruption and graft at City Hall. The things that may have seemed minor in our initial cost-benefit analysis (like politically deceiving the residents and Kim feeling used) in the small context of one single case, loom much larger when considered in the full context of many repeated cases.

Rule-Utilitarianism

The critics who attack utilitarian ethics with extreme examples of conflict between utilitarianism and strong ethical convictions or conventional moral rules can also be answered as follows. What is the basis for the conventional moral rules that most people in a society adhere to? Why do these rules exist, and why do most people obey them?

It is important to define what is meant by the conventional moral rules. These are the classic moral rules that have stood the test of time over the centuries. They are the type of rules that we find in the Ten Commandments against killing, stealing

33

and lying (but excluding the purely pious commandments such as the prohibition against graven images).

A simple answer is that the conventional moral rules have long existed, and are widely followed, because they are useful. They are useful because they have benefits that are clearly greater than their costs to society as a whole. That means that these moral rules exist in the first place for utilitarian reasons. Then the conventional moral rules cannot be in conflict with that very same utilitarian approach to ethics which originally brought the moral rules into being.

Therefore utilitarianism can simply be practiced by following the usual moral rules. It may not be necessary to calculate and weigh the costs and benefits of each ethical decision. It is usually sufficient to obey the conventional moral rules, so long as this is done in a thoughtful and ethically sensitive manner.

Of course some rules that have been accepted for centuries may not be ethical, and should be changed. We need only point to unjust discrimination based on race, gender or national origin as an example. In parts of the world, the belief in the inferiority of women or of non-white races was accepted for centuries, and it took people of conscience and integrity to point out the error and injustice of this belief. In stressing the importance of conventional moral rules, then, we must not exclude the possibility of reforming some of our deeply held convictions. A theory such as Kant's can help us do this. Kant's unqualified demand for respect for persons would, for instance, rule out discrimination based on race, gender and national origin.

Another issue when considering the limitations of the utilitarian approach is that it may not be possible to make reasonable cost-benefit calculations for every decision. First, it is questionable if human beings can calculate the outcomes of all decisions. For example, what value should be placed upon human life? Or what is the cost to a human being of being terrified by a traumatic experience, or of being confined to a wheelchair? Some things defy calculation. Second, some routine or minor decisions simply do not justify calculation. Or some decisions must be made on the spot in emergencies, without time for calculation.

To cover these situations, we often resort to conventional moral rules of thumb. We do not have to calculate in order to refrain from stealing, assault, or rape. We know that these acts are wrong, from the conventional moral rules pointed out above.

Another way of thinking about conventional moral rules is to focus on the difference between act-utilitarianism and rule-utilitarianism. In the twentieth century, some moral philosophers argued that it leads to more accurate ethical results if we perform a cost-benefit analysis of the *rule* an action follows, rather than of the particular *act* in question. In other words: instead of calculating the costs and benefits of this particular act (for instance, an act of lying in order to help someone), one should calculate the costs and benefits of the rule behind the action (for instance, "I will lie if it helps someone"). These differing positions are known as "act-utilitarianism" and "rule-utilitarianism".

We leave the fine points of "act-utilitarianism" versus "rule-utilitarianism" to the experts. However, the rule-utilitarian approach is useful for us to bear in mind. We recall that our original approach was act-utilitarian, using cost-benefit analysis on an act by act basis. This did not always give us an answer, unless we could find a Pareto-optimal solution, or a solution in which the benefits clearly outweighed the costs, no matter how one looked at it. Now a rule-utilitarian approach provides us with another alternative in a difficult case. Let's try it out by returning Kim and City Hall again.

If Kim accepts the consulting assignment, is she breaking a conventional moral rule? Yes. She would be conspiring with City Hall to deceive the City residents over the amount of the consulting fee. This is joining in a lie. Lying breaks a conventional moral rule, and therefore it is unethical. It is not ethical for Kim to accept the offer according to the rule utilitarian approach.

What about the whistle blowing? Say Kim does nothing about the Mayor's request that she inflate her invoice to fund his activities? From the act-utilitarian approach, the taxpayers bear a cost and receive no offsetting benefit. Then a Pareto-optimal solution does not exist. Given the apparent pattern of inflating the fees of consultants to fund the Mayor's activities, Kim's failure to blow the whistle would help to facilitate this pattern. Thus, using the act-utilitarian approach, we could say that it is unethical for her to ignore the incident.

From the rule-utilitarian approach, would Kim be breaking a conventional moral rule by ignoring the incident? It seems that this is in fact the case. The Mayor is, in effect, stealing taxpayer money to advance his own personal ambition, and she would be making herself an accomplice to theft if she did nothing. The conventional moral rule against theft would be broken, and therefore, from the rule-utilitarian point of view, it is also unethical for Kim to ignore the incident.

Utilitarianism and Kant

We have now explored two different ethical systems, Kant's categorical imperative and the utilitarian approach. Several issues need consideration. First, why do we need more than one ethical theory; why is one not sufficient?

One of the standards that we set for an ethical framework to be useful in making business decisions was that it must be generally accepted by the mainstream of moral philosophers. But there is no single ethical system that is generally accepted as supreme among moral philosophers. Our two main ethical systems, the Kantian approach and utilitarianism, are nevertheless widely respected and often applied. That is why we selected them.

To be sure, using two systems is more cumbersome than one. But there are also advantages in using more than one. These advantages are:

1. Ethics can be a most difficult and demanding area, as we have seen. Therefore, using more than one system can illuminate aspects of problems that may not be as apparent under just a single approach;

2.   Ethical systems simply cannot attain the precision that theories may achieve in the more exact sciences. But this does not mean that ethical reflection is pointless: careful thought will lead us to *better* answers, if not to a unique, unanimously accepted answer. To lead us to *better* answers it is helpful to have two imprecise and incomplete ethical systems than just one imprecise and incomplete system;

3.   In seeking guidance for a difficult decision, we are reassured that we have sound results if more than one system leads to the same choice;

4.   If the systems lead to conflicting results, the issue is likely to be thorny, as we saw in the case of Kim and the whistle blowing dilemma. By carefully analyzing why each system gives a different answer, we may find an error in the way one of the systems has been applied. Otherwise we can concentrate our attention on the most crucial ethical issues.

In regard to point #4, recall that, at first, the Kantian framework and the utilitarian approach gave us conflicting answers for the case of Kim and City Hall. It was only when we pushed the utilitarian analysis a step further that we found that it then agreed with the Kantian approach and indicated that Kim should refuse the consulting assignment.

For simplicity, should one of the systems be the principal one that we use? There need not be a preferred system in order to make sound decisions. Each system has its own strengths and weaknesses. It may be useful to think of our two main systems as the two blades of a single pair of scissors. The scissors will cut best when both blades are used together.

If the systems give different answers, and we re-analyze as suggested, and the answers still differ, what then? This should happen rarely. But if it does, these comments may be helpful. First, some moral philosophers believe that Kant's approach is the more conservative, strict and less compromising. This makes it the more safe and dependable choice, if in doubt.

Similarities or Differences?

The moral philosophers spend much effort disputing between ethical systems. That is what experts should do in a complex field. It locates errors and exposes flawed arguments. We will gratefully let the experts do this useful job for us.

More to our purpose is to explore how and where our two main theories are similar. Their most evident similarity is the principle of <u>universality,</u> which is the base of both systems. Kant's categorical imperative is based on universal law or, equivalently, respect for all persons. Utilitarianism is also built upon universality. It considers the costs and the benefits to *all* persons, not just ourselves. In both systems we recognize universality in the form of conventional moral rules.

Universality is the opposite of only considering one's own interests. A "me first" attitude denies universality because it puts others second. This does not mean that it is always unethical to act on self-interest. But it can be unethical in certain cases, as we shall now see.

Universality and Economics

Adam Smith, was both a professor of moral philosophy and economist. He is famed for pointing out that businesspeople, acting out of pure self-interest, will provide the allocation of economic resources that is most efficient for society as a whole:

"Every individual endeavors to employ his capital so that its produce may be of greatest value. He generally nether intends to promote the public interest, nor knows how much he is promoting it. He intends only his own security, only his own gain. And he is in this led by an INVISIBLE HAND to promote an end which was no part of his intention. By pursuing his own interest, he frequently promotes that of society more effectually than when he really intends to promote it."

"It is not from the benevolence of the butcher, the brewer, or the baker that we expect our dinner, but from their regard for their own self interest."[1]

It is important to add that Adam Smith's conclusion requires that in any particular case, there must be no externalities involved. Externalities are the effects of a decision on someone who is not directly involved in the transaction. An externality imposes either a cost or a benefit to the uninvolved party. For example,

---

[1] Adam Smith, *The Wealth of Nations*, ed. Edwin Cannan (New York, NY: Bantam, 2003).

1.	No self-interested businessperson would build a public road for profit. The reason is that there is no way to collect a fee from the autos using the road. Autos that refuse to pay cannot be cut off from using the road (unless of course it is a toll highway). This benefit to autos that refuse to pay makes them free riders, profiting from an externality of the public road;

2.	A firm that pollutes the air, electric or land creates an externality of pollution whose cost falls on the people exposed to it, whether or not they do business with the firm.

Some externalities involve private persons causing public benefits, as in the case of the public road. Therefore they will not be voluntarily provided to the public by a business acting in its own self-interest. Even though roads are needed, business will have no profit motive to provide them. That is why Adam Smith had to exclude externalities from his conclusion that the pursuit of individual self-interest will always benefit society as a whole.

Externalities also involve private persons causing public costs, as in the case of the polluter.

The polluter does not bear all the costs of his or her activities. Thus, his or her pursuit of self-interest will not necessarily benefit society as a whole.

Economics, Externalities and Ethics

Externalities arise when private persons create public costs. The same thing happens when ethics are based on self-interest alone: other persons may be forced to pay a cost. This cost consists of the interference in their lives that takes place without their consent. For example, an industrial firm creates air and water pollution while manufacturing its product. The manufacturer was simply, and selfishly, attempting to manufacture a product as cheaply as possible. It was not deliberately trying to spread poisons and diseases. But, even though the damage to the surrounding population was unintentional, those unfortunately affected by it are just as sick as if it had been intentional. The damage was inflicted on the environment on account of the manufacturer's selfish behavior.

Externalities cannot all be eliminated in real life. Thus self-interest alone is not sufficient to guarantee ethical behavior under either the Kantian theory or utilitarianism. That is why the basic principle of universality is included in both of these ethical systems to avoid the costs to other parties of moral externalities that may arise from self-interest.

BookHolders.com

Dear Christopher Malcolm,

Thank you for your order. We've listed the books you've purchased below. If you have any questions please email: support@bookholders.com. Enjoy your purchase!

BookHolders.com Customer Support

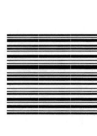

Amazon.com Order #:102-4450085-2145022

****

Order# 46045786
Order Date: 6/23/2012 1:00:16 PM

SKU	Description
2812-767	Ethics Made Easy
C: 408 S: 6A LOC: R	

Individual and Social Ethics

Stealing is wrong because the thief, acting on self-interest, interferes without consent in the life of the victim. This is an unethical act by one individual against another. But there is more involved here than an ethical issue between two individuals. Stealing breaks a conventional moral rule. As we have explained, conventional moral rules can be justified on the basis that they benefit society as a whole. It seems then that stealing, by breaking a conventional moral rule, is harmful to society as a whole. Why?

Stealing conflicts directly with the social institution of private ownership of property. Private property ownership is a valuable social institution because it motivates persons to be as productive as possible, in the expectation that they will profit from their efforts. Society benefits from their productivity. Without secure property rights, people could not buy and sell property because the seller would be unable to give good title to the buyer. In the absence of secure property rights, trade would grind to a standstill. Profits arising from trade would vanish. So secure property rights are the very foundation of a free economy and the profit system.

45

Individuals gaining profit from their efforts invest these profits in all forms of property such as real estate, stocks, bonds, autos, personal belongings, and many other items. Their acquisition of property increases savings and consumption in the economy. The extra consumption adds to business profits which, combined with the extra personal savings, supply capital for business to invest in productive assets. The added investment raises productivity yet more.

All of these benefits flow from the institution of private property. But stealing is a direct attack against private property ownership. If stealing became widespread, even the most effective and well-financed police force could not wipe it out. It would obliterate capitalism and could conceivably destroy society.

Widespread stealing, therefore, would discourage individuals from accumulating property. This would weaken their urge to be as productive as possible. The society loses the benefit of their productivity. This is why society puts a high value upon the right to own private property, and has a moral rule against stealing.

For compelling pragmatic reasons, society requires us to obey the rule against stealing, as well as the other conventional moral rules. These rules benefit us all, and are our shared moral property.

And when the conventional moral rules break down we all are seriously injured.

The moral fabric of a society is based on human cooperation, and it is in our joint and several interests that we follow and uphold the conventional moral rules. We are social creatures, and community is itself a good since it allows us to flourish and thrive. Upholding this community through following just rules is thus also good. Part of evaluating a decision is assessing whether it promotes life in the community by respecting others and their needs.

The Role of Law

Of course, modern societies do not rely solely upon each citizen's coming to the conclusion that each individual's conforming to conventional moral rules is best for the community at large. Externalities illustrate that trusting each citizen to sacrifice self-interest for the good of the whole may be misplaced trust. Thus, modern societies have codified most of the conventional moral rules as laws and have provided sanctions and punishments for their violation.

In many cases, therefore, individualized ethical analysis and cost-benefit calculation may be dispensed with, not just because there may not be time or the calculation may be too complex, but because the law provides a solution and *imposes* it upon us. Although this may appear arbitrary, and deprive us of individual freedom, these conclusions ignore the foundation and derivation of much of the law. On the contrary, the law is generally a codification of those very conventional moral rules which underpin the ethical theories we have discussed above. These rules have survived for centuries because they have worked and are good for society as a whole. But, as we noted earlier, there are times when the law and ethics part company and we need to be aware of this possibility.

<u>An Ethical Framework</u>

To conclude, the above analysis demonstrates that the philosophical traditions we have discussed—Kant, utilitarianism, and Smith—generally agree on the rules of ethical behavior. The disagreements are usually about the philosophical justification supporting each theory. This is a matter of serious concern to philosophers, but it is less important to users of the theories. In short, having chosen prescriptive ethical theories which are not only generally accepted by mainstream philosophy but which we have shown are closely interrelated to each other and the law, we are ready to propose a framework which fulfills the standards we set for ourselves at the beginning of this essay. Although we have derived the prescriptive framework from philosophical and ethical foundations for the purpose of guiding individuals to ethical decisions, we would strongly suggest that much of the framework would be equally useful for the making of any significant decision. The framework is as follows:

The Decision-Making Framework

The basis for "ethical decision making" begins with a good decision-making process. Hence, the method that is presented here begins with generic steps that are necessary for any effective decision making process. The issue of ethics becomes most relevant to this method as one is evaluating different decision alternatives. Just as we must use different evaluation criteria (i.e. net present value, strategic priority, time to market, feasibility, etc.) when evaluating different decision alternatives, we must also include ethical criteria in this evaluation process. The following decision making method highlights how ethical perspectives can be integrated into an effective decision making process.

By using this decision making framework, we will integrate ethical perspectives into our existing knowledge regarding decision making. This framework will also help us learn to identify ethical issues that may not be obvious at first sight. Employing this framework does not guarantee that we will always choose the most ethical solution.

But it will greatly help us to get closer to that ideal result. Here are the steps to follow:

1. **Issue Identification**

- Identify the decisions and issues that are involved.
- Determine if there are associated ethical issues. Ask how this decision/action will affect others? Is there something wrong personally, interpersonally, or socially here? Define and state the ethical issues as clearly as possible. It may be useful to state these issues as questions that focus on the ethical implications of the decisions.

2. **Information Gathering**

- Gathering information and facts that are relevant to a decision may be more difficult than it seems as information may be unavailable and/or ambiguous.
- A critical step in gathering information is to identify the affected stakeholders and determine their interests, values and opinions.
- Information also needs to be gathered about any legal requirements of the decision.

3. Consider Alternatives

- Carefully develop a variety of alternative courses of action.
- Consider as many feasible alternatives as practically possible.

4. Evaluate Alternatives From Various Perspectives

1. Prior to evaluating the alternatives, decision makers must first identify the evaluation criteria that will be used to choose a course of action. There are a range of standard "business" criteria that can be used such as net present value, strategic priority, long-term versus short-term business needs, feasibility, sustainability, resource allocation issues, time to market, etc. In addition to these "business" criteria, one also wants to use the following ethical criteria to evaluate the decision.

5. Apply ethical evaluation criteria

a) <u>Which alternative respects the rights and dignity of the stakeholders and can be universally applied?</u>
   - For each alternative, apply Kant's categorical imperative both in the form of:
     1. A universal law; and

2. Respect for persons.
- For each decision alternative, identify the ramifications if everyone were to follow the principle that underlies that alternative. For each decision alternative, determine if you are respecting the stakeholders and not treating them merely as objects.

b) <u>Which alternative will produce the most good and the least harm?</u>
  - Apply the utilitarian perspective to analyze each of the decision alternatives.
  - For each alternative, identify the costs and benefits to the stakeholders (see Table 2).
  - Weigh the costs and benefits of each alternative and determine if there is a solution that is Pareto-optimal (meaning a solution that promotes the greatest good for the greatest number of people, with no loss or harm to anyone).
  - If there is no Pareto-optimal alternative, choose the alternative that produces the most benefits and causes the least harm to the stakeholders.

c) <u>Do any of the alternatives violate a conventional moral rule?</u>
   - For each alternative, apply the rule-utilitarian approach by checking to see if it would violate a conventional moral rule. These are the types of rules that we find in many great religious traditions, such as rules against killing, stealing, and lying.
   - How would you feel if your actions were reported on the front page of the Wall Street Journal?

d) <u>Resolve Conflicting Answers</u>
   - If the three ethical approaches in step 4 produced conflicting answers, try to determine which of the approaches seems most relevant to your particular situation.
   - In evaluating alternatives, you also want to consider if any of the alternatives are illegal or are required by law. Determining that an alternative is illegal should lead to its rejection, while determining that an alternative is

legally required should lead to its adoption.

6. Making a Decision With Ethical Perspectives

- In determining which decision making alternative to choose, you will have to weigh the results of the different decision making criteria. One alternative may have the greatest NPV, while another alternative may be the most strategically advantageous, while another may be the most ethical. The challenge is for you to find the decision that produces the most business value in an ethical way.

- Evaluate your preliminary decision by revisiting each of the four ethical approaches you used in step 4 and rate your confidence in your decision (see Table 3).

7. Propose a Convincing Ethical Decision

- You need to be able to explain to others that you have weighed the ethical issues involved and have made the *most* ethical decision possible.

- You also need to explain to others that you have followed a process that is as ethical as possible.

8. Reflect on the Ethics of Your Decision

- How well did you do at assessing the ethical impact of your decision? What do you need to do differently next time?

Note. Answers to many of the toughest ethical issues you will face in business and in life will depend on what standards and tests you apply. That does not mean that standards and tests are arbitrary or useless. Even if you decide that a test does not help in a particular situation, considering it can nonetheless be important in helping you understand the reasons you have chosen as you have. Furthermore, for many decisions you will not have the luxury to take the time to follow this process to determine all the ethical ramifications of your decision. However, if you use this process when you do have time it will quickly become part of the useful knowledge you carry with you as you make quick decisions.

IDENTIFYING CONSEQUENCES TO STAKEHOLDERS

	Decision Alternative #1	Decision Alternative #2	Decision Alternative #3	Decision Alternative #4
STAKEHOLDERS	**POSSIBLE CONSEQUENCES OF EACH ALTERNATIVE ON EACH STAKEHOLDER**			
1.				
2.				
3.				
4.				
5.				
6.				

Notes:

1. When identifying stakeholders think about owners, managers, customers, employees, suppliers, different aspects of the community, the government, the natural environment, and of course stockholders. Try to think as broadly as you can about possible stakeholders as you may also need to include future generations and people who are one step removed from the immediate stakeholders.
2. Determine the relative level of importance of different stakeholders.
3. In thinking about consequences, you should focus on those consequences that have a particularly high probability of occurring. In thinking about consequences make sure you look at both long-term and short term consequences as well as real versus symbolic consequences (what message does your action send).
4. Finally, use your analysis to determine which decision alternative will produce the greatest good for the greatest number of people.

ETHICAL EVALUATION OF
ALTERNATIVE DECISIONS

DECISION ....

ETHICAL DECISION-MAKING EVALUATION CRITERIA Scoring: 5 is the most positive and 1 is the least positive response.	Score 1-5
1. Have I/we thought broadly about any ethical issues associated with the decision that have to be made?	
2. Have I/we involved as many as possible of those who have a right to have input to, or actual involvement in, making this decision and action-plan?	
3. Does this decision respect the rights and dignity of the stakeholders?	
4. Can this decision be universally applied?	
5. Does this decision produce the most good and the least harm to the relevant stakeholders?	
6. Does this decision uphold relevant conventional moral rules?	
7. Can I live with this decision if it is reported on the TV news?	
8. Does this decision enable me to develop character traits that allow me to live with myself and others peacefully?	

What is the total of all of the scores? _____

If the total is below 32 revisit your decision and action-plan.

About the Author

Les Livingstone is an MBA Program Director at a leading online university. He earned MBA and Ph.D. degrees at Stanford University and is a CPA (licensed in NY and TX).

Since 1991 he has directed his own consulting firm, which specializes in Damage Estimation for large-scale Commercial Litigation and in Business Valuation. He has served as a Consulting or Testifying Expert in many cases, including Breach of Contract, Patent Infringement, Fraudulent Conveyance, Antitrust, Dealer Termination, Franchise Disputes, and Securities Fraud. He has testified in Federal and State courts in Arizona, California, Florida, Georgia, Illinois, New York, Massachusetts, Rhode Island, and Texas, and he has also testified before Federal government agencies including the FTC, FERC, as well as the Public Utilities Commission of Texas.

His previous experience in accounting, finance and business includes the following:

- Babson College: Professor of Accounting and Chairman, Division of Accounting & Law.

- The MAC Group (since acquired by Cap Gemini/Ernst & Young Consulting), an international management consulting firm specializing in design and implementation of business strategy for major corporations: Principal.

- PricewaterhouseCoopers, an international accounting firm: Partner.

- Georgia Institute of Technology: Fuller E. Callaway Professor of Accounting.

- Ohio State University: Arthur Young Distinguished Professor of Accounting.

Publications: Author or coauthor of:

- About 50 articles in leading professional journals.
- Numerous chapters in authoritative handbooks.
- Recent books available on amazon.com are:

1. Economics Made Easy, (2nd Edition) 2011

2. Ethics Made Easy, (2nd Edition) 2011

3. Finance Made Easy, (2nd Edition) 2011

4. Common Sense, 2011

5. The Economics of Public Choice, 2010

6. Ethical Decision Making, 2009

7. The Economics of Energy, 2008

8. Guide to Business Valuation, 2007

9. "The Portable MBA in Finance and Accounting", John Wiley & Sons, Inc., Hoboken, NJ, 4th edition, 2009. Selection of the Book of the Month Club, the Fortune Book Club and the Money Book Club. Later, the paperback edition was a selection of the Quality Paperback Book Club. Translated into Chinese, French, German, Indonesian, Japanese, Portuguese, Russian and Spanish.

Web Page: http://leslivingstone.com/

Made in the USA
Lexington, KY
04 January 2012